PRiCkLY

Prickly

Poems by

Mather Schneider

NⱲY Books™

The New York Quarterly Foundation, Inc.
New York, New York

NYQ Books™ is an imprint of The New York Quarterly Foundation, Inc.

The New York Quarterly Foundation, Inc.
P. O. Box 2015
Old Chelsea Station
New York, NY 10113

www.nyq.org

First Edition

Set in New Baskerville

Layout by Christina Sinibaldi and Raymond P. Hammond

Cover Design by Dave Bates

Cover illustration by Mather Schneider

Author Photograph by Mather Scneider

Library of Congress Control Number: 2017941261

ISBN: 978-1-63045-041-0

For Ara

Contents

Prickly

ALEJANDRINA GARCIA

How many times did I drive you in my cab
to your kidney dialysis, Alejandrina?
3 times a week for 2 years, Jesus
how many mornings at 5
I'd creep into your parking lot
and you'd come stumbling out of your apartment
number 401,
sleepy but cheerful
smiling in the face of hopelessness
with your old blue blanket and worn out pillow
that you always carried to dialysis
so you could sleep in the chair
while the machine cleaned you.

45 years old.

Now you've died and I have an empty space
at 5 o'clock in the morning
and I keep thinking of you
how we'd drive those dark streets from the south side
usually quiet, not talking much
what was there
to say?
I would have the radio on, music
or some news of the world
some terrible news of the world that didn't mean much
to a cab driver
or to a woman so sick she couldn't drink a glass of water
even when it was 110 degrees
in this desert summer.

Summer, winter, fall, spring
I drove you
and I knew the smell of you, like medicine
and bed clothes
and your hair brown and messy

and your face swollen from the retained liquid
from the food you ate.

Why didn't you kill yourself?
I guess because of your grandchildren
who you told me about once
and your daughter even though you fought with her
and sometimes you went out with a friend
but no man, no man
for years.

It was only a 15 minute trip
from your apartment to the dialysis center.
I would go out to Valencia, make a U turn
and then go back and merge onto the freeway
for a couple of miles, get off
at Ajo and then wait at that stupid traffic light
that never wanted to change
and sometimes I'd just run it, no cops
both of us feeling absurd
sitting there at a red light
the only car on the streets anywhere
sometimes I'd just run it and you'd
chuckle and it would give us both
a little thrill, like we had cheated
fate somehow, but just a
little

but most times I'd wait
for the damn thing to go to green
afraid of getting a ticket
and losing my job
my sacred job, my meal ticket
the job I needed, still need, the job I love
and hate, my curse,
my way.

I miss you Alejandrina.
I always thought
you might just be better off dead
and I thought the same about myself
but I don't think
that way anymore.

I wish I could have another early morning
with you, even if we didn't say
a word, I wish I could
drop you off one more time
at the dialysis center
and watch you waddle toward the lit up doors
where your seat waited
like my seat waits for me
the sun still a long way from coming up
to peek over the Rincon Mountains
and lay its pitiless
beautiful rays upon us.

SARGE'S POEM

Eating free bags of popcorn
at the bar.

Sand bags
for beer.

UNDER THE PURPLE UMBRELLA

I'm given an address that doesn't exist
from the computer on the dash of the cab.
I call the phone number.

"Hello?" A man's voice, wind
thick in the mouthpiece.

"Hello, this is Matt, your cab driver," I say. "Where
are you exactly?"

"I'm on 29th Street," he says. "I'm about a hundred
yards from a big building that is under
construction,
I'm sitting under a tree
in the shade, purple shirt,
blue jeans,
you can't miss me."

I whip off the freeway
and see him there, waving.
He gets up from the dirt
with his pack, stumbles toward my cab.
He's about 60 years old, messy hair, sunburnt.
He gets in, the smell
of fecal matter following.

"How's it going?" he says.

"All right," I say, rolling
down the window.

"Take me to the bus station, will ya pal? It won't cost
more than 10 bucks will it, that's
all I got."

"No problem."

"Hey," he says, "Did you know Denny's
will give you a free breakfast
on your birthday? And they don't
even check your ID! It's not your
birthday, is it?"

"No."

"Shit, it don't matter! They won't
even check! And at IHOP
they give you a big ice cream
sundae on your birthday.
And at Big Jack's BBQ
too, free sandwich on your birthday."

"You got the bases covered," I say.

"You like baseball?"

"Sure."

"Who's your team?"

"Diamondbacks."

"Hey, did you know when the Diamondbacks score
more than 6 runs in a game, you get 2 free
tacos at Taco Bell? All you got to do
is buy a soda."

"No shit? They scored 7 last night."

"Hell, then, let's go to Taco Bell! It's on me!"

We both laugh at that one.

"That reminds me," he says.
"I've got batting practice
later with the Sidewinders
over in Corbett Field. You know
where that is right?"

"Yeah, sure."

"You want some free tickets? I got free tickets,
just give me a call sometime,
anytime!"

"Will do, my man."

As we approach the city bus station, he points
to the sidewalk.

"There's Tony," he says. "I'm gonna help him sell
hot dogs
from his hot dog stand."

"Where?"

"Right there, under the purple umbrella!"

I look at the sidewalk, see some people walking,
rushing here, rushing there,
no hot dog stand, no purple umbrella.

"I see him."

I pull to the curb. He holds out
a ten dollar bill
that looks like it had once
been part of a bird's nest.

"Just keep it, man."

Without hesitating
he stuffs it back in his pocket.

"I'll be expecting that call," he says,
"anytime, my brother, free tickets! You got
my number, right?"

"I got it."

He gets out of the cab with his pack
and I ease away.
When I look again
he's gone.

I'll be 50 in
what, 4 months?

Hard to believe
any of this.

I turn right on 18th and take
the back way
to Taco Bell.

THE LADIES AT FOOD CITY

The ladies stand outside Food City
waiting for their cabs.

No cab driver wants to pick them up.
No cab driver wants to help them
with their groceries
and then drive them a mile or two
to their tiny apartments
and help them get the groceries
out again.
No cab driver wants to stand there
in the heat with them.
No cab driver wants to climb their steps
and then take their 4 or 5 or 6
crumpled dollar bills.

The ladies stand in front of Food City
eyes following every cab
that rolls down the street
hoping it's the one.
They stand there while their lettuce wilts
and their milk sours.
They stand there sweating in the 100 degree heat
because they know if they wait inside the store
they might miss their cab,
they know no cab driver will take the trouble
to get out to look for them,
they know they are
not worth it.

They don't talk to each other
as they stand there
in the stingy shade.
They are jealous when another's cab
gets there first
and sometimes they get in arguments
over whose cab is whose.

The ladies outside Food City
look lonely and ashamed
knowing that they should be able to rely
on their daughters or sons or husbands
but they can't.
They never thought they'd end up
like this
standing in the sun
leaning on their grocery carts
broke and bent
in their house dresses and old shoes
with dry skin
and gray hair.

But there they are:
black, white, Mexican, Chinese...

It isn't much, but it does warm you
the way they light up
just a bit
when you drive your taxi over
roll the window down
and say their name.

THE ROOFERS

She always wanted me
to get the roof fixed.
It leaked for years.

They came today
got right to work, I had to love that sense
of purpose.
I watched them for a while, then felt like a fool
and came inside,
listened to the boots walking
all over my world,
the house shaking like a war
for hours,
me down here in my bunker,
dust falling from the ceiling
and them up there
in the open,
fearless,
balanced like little GI Joe dolls
on the edge of a bathtub
filled with hot tar, the hot tar

they mopped onto the surface
like heaven under
a black light
the stink of it, the nasty stink of it.

By late afternoon it quieted down.
I heard them laughing, and one guy
sweeping up my patio
like he owned the place, like some filthy
shopkeeper, whistling
a child's tune

and when they drove their huge truck away
they didn't even say goodbye.

I came outside,
leaned my ladder against the house
and climbed up,
peeking my head up like a survivor
looking onto a quiet sunset
over a battle field.

It looks pretty good, but what
do I know?

I thought, shit, a 4 followed
by 3 zeros

and I thought,
she still isn't
coming back

and I thought,
now it will probably never fucking rain
again.

COWGIRL

"He had a dick
like a horse,"
she said, speaking
of her last lover. "It
was way too big."

"I thought the bigger the
better?" I said.

"Well," she
sighed, "up to
a point,
but yours is
much better, much more
suitable."

"Great," I said. "What
luck."

We were lying
in bed.

"Let's change
the subject,"
I said.

But she didn't
seem to
hear me.

Her body
was there
but her mind was
somewhere else.

Probably
at the fucking
rodeo.

MARCOS MENDIVIL

He limps out of his broken down adobe house
with a smile like an old mule
dusty in the sun
his body contorted and failing.
25 years ago his brother-in-law shot him with a shotgun
from 5 feet away
straight into the gut.

It's ok, he tells me in the taxi
I deserved it
I was an asshole
for a long time I had ideas about revenge
but I've made peace.
I've lived a good life
you have to learn to forgive
though it ain't easy.

A miracle you didn't die,
I say.

The Spirits had other plans for me, he says.

He lives on the Papago reservation
with his Indian wife
she and all their family alcoholics
hanging on by the skin of their teeth
in a destroyed world
his son a troubled
soul with shaved head
and tats all
over him.

Marcos says,
You can't tell that kid nothin'
he's full of hate
but I can't blame him
his mother and I, well

we didn't love him the way
we should have.

He turns away
like he sees someone he knows on the street
but there's no one there

and then he goes on:
But I have two beautiful granddaughters
who I thank God for every day
they think I'm a hero
they're so young they don't know anything yet
I just hope they get off the rez
before it's too late.

I take him to the doctor
and when I pick him up to take him home
he has X-rays the doctor gave him.
He holds them up to the light
of the cab window.

There's my kidney stones, he points
and all that there
that's the buckshot
still inside me.

I look at the buckshot
stars against the black background
of his flesh,
pin pricks in his soul,
bones curved lasers with porous edges,
kidney stones ghostly piranha.

He wants me to know
he's not lying.
He wants to see in my eyes
that I believe
and understand.

FREE-FORM BOLERO

We cat nopalitos
for lunch
pruned from our hard yard

and we love the afternoon away
both of us hunter
both of us prey

then sleep.

I dream about pueblos
with names of women
and a smoky cantina with flowered curtains
and ironwood tables
polished by a million brown elbows.

The floor fan blows the hair on my legs
whispers chicken skin goodbyes
to my sweat
and as the heat rises with the finale of April
I am at peace with what will come:

wormy compost of May
foul-smelling hat
sunburned deeds
mesquite syrup and cactus jelly
sealed in jars like preserved lust

the throat-burning flames of bacanora June
sour stains of July
lime and onion tears
of August

the desert stretched out like an endless
mockery of self-importance.

Funneled into the triumph
of now

the sun floats down
a popped balloon at a gala ball

and as I wake up
it's like I'm face to face
with the prettiest girl
at the last dance of the world

and she's looking at me
like she just woke up too.

CHEWING AN ICY NUT

Another beautiful morning
of arrows and boleros

beer cans scattered in the yard
like the wedding car
crashed.

Another beautiful morning
of iced white wine
and nihilism
memories like still-deaths
cigarettes and sore bones and Mexico
whispering like the nearly impossible past
of a soft Indian girl
with slender arms and heat-waves

singeing the edges
of the curtains
tinted with significance.

I peek out like a ground squirrel
chewing an icy nut
farther than I ever thought I'd get
from that iffy beginning.

Sometimes you go years thinking
all the good days are over
but then they come again

and they come with a vengeance.

GUTTER PUNK

A pitch black tattoo
covers almost her entire head.
Only a lightning streak of white
is left on her right cheek
like something frozen in an act of violence.

It obliterates her.

Ugly people look at her
and hate her
for doing to herself
what nature did to them
because underneath you can see
she had been a pretty girl.
They look at her like a cripple
would look at someone
mutilating her own leg.

Beautiful people look at her
and silently feel superior

and even the heavily tattooed bikers
are at a loss for words.

She is marked forever
by all the pain and confusion of youth
turned inside out

and her eyes peek out of the blackness
like dew on an early grave.

DIGGING FOR THE GOLDEN ADDRESS

A truck beeps backing up
in the Pep Boys parking lot, traffic is a stripped screw

on Fairmount Stravenue, a bum coughs
behind a bank's dumpster, a fare winks at me

(a number on the computer screen)
in my taxi, I twist

the key that makes the motor jump, feel the meaninglessness
of stress, hear the music of tires riding

the radio, flip a bitch, dig
for the golden address, then the crunch

of footsteps to my cab, the secular
Hello, the How ya doin', the Where you goin', the To Hell

if I don't change my ways, the Ha ha,
the No seriously to Oracle

and 8th, the Hurry
please she's waiting, she's pissed,

she's beautiful, the What's
this gonna cost me, the I'm really not

sure, brother,
the breath held in the quiet cut

across three lanes
to veer south, two hearts beating

together, like two lovers who have come
to hate each other, the rise

and fall of laughter in the window of the car
next to us at the stop light.

The sun seems so silent
but must be deafening up close, a drunken god

snoring a fiery dream of what might
as well be forever, then the squeaky

brakes of arrival, the sound of dollars
in my palm, like leaves landing

on the ground, old leaves with faces
of dead men, the relief

of moving on, the light of a smoke. And time
you can hear it passing

on all sides, air pushing against the inside
of a tire, my whisper

Oh god when a small boy
crawls out of a cardboard box

in the middle of the street, the squeals
as he runs towards his mother, his mother

on her cell phone on the sidewalk, the mute
tremble of her lips

into it, the horns
the horns the horns

of this debacle of a band, all trying to
outblow the other, the wind a ring-tone

of a Tohono O'Odham ghost, fingers fumbling
for the wrong switch, windshield wipers insane

on dry glass, like arms pleading
for everything to just stop

but it doesn't stop,
it never stops,

only the pleading
stops.

NOT TODAY, MR. POTTER

The old man has fingernails
like a mummy
and he's fighting with the nurse as she brings him out
of the assisted-living place
and tries to put him in my cab

long white beard
body wiry as a demon
shoulder blades swiveling beneath
a torn yellow t-shirt.

I am supposed to take him
to the doctor.

She opens the cab door and it is like trying
to get a cat into a bathtub
he clings to the sides of the cab
kicks at her
tries to scratch her.

Maybe he'll like the front seat better?
The nurse says to me

but he doesn't like the front any better

and then he starts to screech
like some kind of blood-thirsty
dinosaur-bird.

Uh, I say to her, You are coming with us
right?

Oh, no she says, he's ALL YOURS!

Now come ON, Mr. Potter, she says, let's
be GOOD TODAY!

At this moment he turns to me and grins
with brown teeth that look like they've been
sharpened by a Congolese chisel
and swings that old wrinkled red claw
with those long filthy fingernails
toward my face.

I jump out of the cab, say to the lady,

I AIN'T takin' this guy anywhere! Get him
out of here!

She looks at me like she could break me in half
with her mason forearms and hot dog fingers
shakes her head and
leads him away.

The old man looks back at me
with a

"We'll meet again one day"

sparkle in his marbled peepers.

HAROLD'S STORY

Harold's a librarian at the prison
on South Wilmot
and at The Bambi he was telling me the story
about a female librarian who used to work with him
and how she got caught
fucking an inmate in the library.

They fired her ass
but the clincher is she waited
until the man got out of prison
and then married him
which just tore Harold up.

It had happened years ago
but still he trembled with rage
at the thought of it
like he just wanted to kill this guy
and the woman too.

I drank my beer
wondering why it bothered him so much

as if some people don't deserve love
or a second chance
as if it was just not right somehow

and when Harold's wife came back from the bathroom
and sat down
it was like there was bullet-proof glass

between them.

MIRRORS AND STORMS

My wife's old Yaqui granny
put blankets over the mirrors
when it rained.

I think of this in my cab
stuck on the shoulder of Mission Road
during a monsoon storm
windshield wipers flapping like the arms of a hiker
in a swarm of bees.

I keep glancing at myself in the rearview mirror
my face twisted
and shadowy.

It's too much
in the middle of all this.
That isn't me,
something else is coming through.

I put a handkerchief over the mirror
sit here in my little island cave
of metal and rubber

looking out at the lightning and rain
like atomic bombs blowing up
all over the known world.

OUR HOUSE

In the morning the living
room is flooded with light

and the back room is cold, like a tomb
but in the evening the back room is then flooded

with light, and the living room
is shadowed, and gives your hands

a clammy feel, and like
ghosts are swimming in unresolved

dilemmas, unfinished futures, and so we gather
with the sun, and we follow it like flowers

with long necks, and at night
we dream the same dream

with its trillion arms
and legs and heads

and we jerk as if strange beings
are landing on our skin

and all our plans become perfect
in their nonsense.

LITTLE BRIDGES OVER STREAMS

Mohawk Joe shuffled into the Up & Up
where I was sipping a high ball.

"Hey," he said, "I went to the Japanese
garden in Seattle."

"What's that?" I said. "A band?"

"Hell, no," he said, "it's a real garden.
Totally peaceful. Little bridges
over streams. Carefully trimmed and shaped
plants and bushes. That sort of thing.
Very spiritual."

"Spiritual," I said.

"Yeah."

He ordered a beer.
This was our usual place, our normal
sanctuary.

"How big was it?" I said.

"Oh, I don't know…probably
about twice as big
as this place."

His arm swept across the room
and my gaze followed.

I nodded in understanding.
Twice as big as the bar,
our familiar perspective.

Our unit of measurement.

SPEEDWAY AND HOPE

The black metal gate opens when I punch in the code
and I drive my cab in towards the dilapidated
assisted living center.
Slow tires chew the gravel.

He's been watching for me from behind the curtains
and comes wobbling out
50-year-old black guy
with a round smiling face
bloated cheeks
sweat pants and white t-shirt.

He opens the cab door and says:
"You here for me, sir?"

"You John Challet?"

"That's me!"

His leg shakes terribly and he has a hard time
getting into the cab.
It looks like he's had a stroke or two
and who knows what else
but he makes it
and we get going.

"You know where we going, sir?" he says.

"I think so," I say.

"1124 East Speedway," he says. "Speedway and Hope."

"Speedway and Hope?"

"Yeppuh."

He's got a glow about him
accentuated by the warm fall sun.

"What's YOUR name?" he says.

"Matt."

"Nice to meet you Matt, I'm John. John Challet."

"Nice to meet you, John."

"I'm getting married next week," he says.

"Oh, yeah? Congratulations!"

"She's a real beauty, we're gonna stay
with my old pop, I can
finally get out of this place, I done spent
my two years, I'm better now."

"That's great, glad to hear it.
Where's your dad live?"

"Over that way," he gestures
to the south. "He lives in
a castle. Real big."

"Sounds nice."

"You got the sugar diabetes, Matt?"

"Not yet."

"I do, but I don't let it worry me none.
You put a little sugar
under your tongue if you ain't

40

feeling right. Johnny knows
what to do."

Then he starts singing, he just
starts singing in this rough black man's
voice:

"You got to love her like she's the only
ooooonnneee
you got to live each day like it's the last oooooneee
oh, she's my everythinnnngggg
she's my coffee and toast
she found me when I was loooost..."

He sings for 2 or 3 minutes
and when he finishes he says,
"How was that?"

"Beautiful, John."

I cruise down Speedway looking
at the numbers.

Then I see it: HOPE CHARITY HOUSE.
It's a place where they have classes and support groups
for people who need help
because of physical and mental disabilities.

"THIS BE THE PLACE!" he says. "You found it, Matt!"

I pull in and park.

"Look, there's Grant's truck!" he says, pointing
to an old red truck in the parking lot.
"Grant's here!"

The fare is paid for by the state.
He uses both hands
to lift his spasming leg
out of the cab
shuts the door and wobbles toward the building.

Then he turns and waves.

I drive off
humming low

trying not to lose
the melody.

THE SAINT

I once knew a man
who told me he would be willing
to die for me

and when I called him a liar
he punched me in the face.

LET'S NOT

Let's not be melodramatic
let's not wear turtlenecks in the sun
or scuff our boots on purpose
let's not stand at the podium and apologize
for nonexistent stage fright
let's not flaunt our raccoon eyes
or applaud wildly like soccer moms
at kindergarten graduation
or roar that we are poets roaring or that we have tits
or cunts or balls or dicks
let's not be sad because it's cool
or mouth love because it's an easy road to sainthood
let's not be delicate because it's expected
let's not pretend we're Indians
or gangsters or beatniks
or are channeling some Egyptian princess
let's not smoke pot and tag people and gloat
let's not drop names like women purposely drop silken kerchiefs
let's not brag about how much we drank
or read
or scribbled
let's not quote Becket
or carry "outlaw bibles"
or romanticize bus stops
or heroin needles
let's stop saying blood and guts and
let's stop saying genius and must-read.

Let's start being honest
about all this
it's not much
we're not much
goobers in the sand pile
downers in skinny jeans
latte-slurpers and sushi-chewers
screws loose and heads fat as Thanksgiving turkeys

just look at the way we walk and talk and
make videos
it's sickening
even our laughter is false and condescending
our little hard-ons
our rhetorical suffering
our tweedle dumb theories
12 poems about starvation before dinner
9 poems about heart-ache after dinner
cutting our brilliance off in time
for the late show.

Rebels, please, even our preachers have earrings
and tattoos
everybody's trying to sell their penny-sick souls
everybody's trying to sell their dimestore doohickies
how can you not throw up perusing
the cherub faces
of the poor prepubescent world-changers
chapbook staplers
pony-tailed haiku poopers
shopping mall roosters with perfect noses
crowing about the hard life
academics writing papers about reviving the male spirit
or the female spirit
with Facebook photos like real estate agents
slapping their own asses
loafers and tenure and diarrhea down their legs
which nobody will mention
between their cult-chants of togetherness
and spurts of roses and lilac
and communal
iambs.

Where will it end
where can it end

our doggy-whimpers
our parrot inflections
praying for disability or inheritance or grants or awards
or at the very least
pity
writing "you are beautiful" in lipstick on the mirror
believing everything that falls off
the tips of our baby-soft fingers.

NO-SHOW AT THE TRICO SUPER STOP

For a cabby, everything starts with that beep
from the computer monitor on the dash, that tone
from the mother board.
It's like the beep of the flat-liner
but for us it's like the beginning of life, or what
passes for life
and so you punch the ACCEPT button, you've got to accept
everything that's given to you, that's one
of the unwritten rules
and you wait for the address to appear
and sometimes it's some crazy place way
out in the fucking county, 18 miles away, and you get
that engine going and fly
into the sun.

And while you're chewing up the bone-white highway
you feel like you're always chasing
something, like you've been chasing something
your whole life, and it's more than a fare or
a dollar, you don't even know
what it is you're chasing after, maybe
some kind of meaning
to life, some kind of answer,
some unknowable thing in some unknowable place, something
that will help you, something that will
complete you.

And you call up the provided telephone number
as you toe that line between speeding
and jail
and a young girl answers:
"Trico Super Stop, can I help you?"

And you say
"Yes, ma'am, this is Matt with Yellow Taxi, do you
have someone there waiting for a taxi?"

47

"Oh, yes, we do, she's waiting right here."

"Tell her I'll be there soon,
tell her I'm coming!"

And you whip
off the freeway and into the green cotton fields
that they've laid out in the desert, the irrigation
water rushing and gurgling through the fluffy rows
and you pass a man on a tractor leaving tracks of mud
on the road, feeling free and small under the barbarous
blue skies, and you wave and he waves
and you pass farm houses like the one you grew
up in
and long crooked lines
of mailboxes for the people who struggle
somewhere back in the invisible distance,
advancing into the heat waves like silvery gelatin
that slip away when you reach them,
smashing the snakes that have been smashed into the road
already a hundred times,
taking those turns with the yellow warning signs
and thinking of your father telling you at age 8
that a country road is like a woman
because it's got sharp curves
and soft shoulders
and thinking of what he found
at the end of his chase
that he can't tell you about
now.

And you finally see that little gas station store
in the butthole of nowhere, skid
into the parking lot
and immediately get a feeling of doom, it's the moment
of truth and it doesn't feel right.

You get out of the cab dizzy in the blaring rays
go inside the store.

"Taxi!"

And the female cashier who you talked to on the phone
says, "She's waiting outside, she was
just there a minute ago!"

The cashier's a nice girl and checks the bathroom
then follows you outside, searching the sides
of the building
and then even checks around back
as if she might be hiding somewhere
crouching in some shadow.

"She was a nice lady," the cashier says, "She had a
splint on her arm."

"Was she a local?" you ask.

"Never seen her before."

And you both stand there in front looking
at the gas pumps and the empty country road
like all that emptiness inside you, like 50 more
wasted miles, wasted time, wasted gas
and she says

"Look, there's her cup sitting right here!"

And you both look at this big plastic cup
of soda sitting on the ice machine outside
the doors of the Super Stop, sweat
dripping down the sides
like your own face.

"I'm sorry," the cashier says

and you say, "It's all right, it happens."

She goes inside

and you walk over and pick up
that plastic cup,
still full
and still cold.

BIPOLAR POEM FOR A BIPOLAR WORLD

Sometimes you get so high
your face bends

and the clouds are blurry
white-noise at your feet

and you think

this will never end
this can't ever end.

You are a man from earth
your sweat has rotted hats
your knuckles have worn out gloves
you have corroded belt buckles
you have ruined chains
with your drippings

but sometimes
you get so high you feel
clean as a flower
just bloomed from the long
skinny stalk
and you hear the buzz of every bee in the world
waking up

and you quiver to be eaten and
sucked dry
for tomorrow you will push that clock
like a burro turning a water pump slowly in the sun
and tears will rise
ripe and shiny from the mystery

from that deep place people die
to know.

RAY OF SUNSHINE ON A WEDNESDAY AFTERNOON

The round old white lady scowls outside Target
with a plastic bag and 3 house plants.
After we load up, she climbs in my taxi
and starts in:

"Miracle you found the place
here's my ticket you know what that's for right
that means I don't have to pay for the ride
I know you guys aren't that bright
Handicar was much better
I just loved Handicar I can't believe your company got the contract
I used Handicar for years
they were the best
I just loved Jodi and Betsy and Sally in the dispatch office
real sweethearts and they knew what they were doing
not like the morons at your dispatch office
they don't even know Tucson at all
I mean where the hell do they find these idiots
they're RUDE
and they expect you to give them an EXACT ADDRESS
what a pain in the ass
and these drivers ya'll got Jesus Christ
where do you get your drivers an insane asylum
I thought that last driver was gonna murder me
I didn't leave the house for a week afterwards
and I called in on him too
you bet your sweet ass I did
nobody treats me like that and gets away with it
I know my rights
he didn't even know where he was GOING
God damned you're a taxi driver and you don't know where
Calle De Osa is
it's right THERE I mean shit everybody knows that
I just don't know why you guys had to steal the contract
from Handicar
they were the best
I hope you know where you're going
I'd like to get home sometime today
and watch those speed bumps Mario Andretti
my hemorrhoids are acting up."

52

SEASONS GREETINGS

There was a Christmas card in my mailbox
addressed to Suzy Sumner
who must've lived
here before me.

There was no cash inside
only a photo of a family
standing on a beach
wrapped in towels.

It took a minute
before I figured out the mother
reminded me
of Bette Midler.

The handwriting on the card
was girlish
and said it would be good
to see me
in the new year.

For a second I felt
I wasn't who I was
supposed to be

and then like magic
she signed it

"Love,
Everybody."

SEIZURES

On the sandstone patio outside the neuro clinic
there he is
with his shaggy black dog
both of them patient as refugees.
I ease up to the curb
and he climbs into the cab and smiles,
says, "Come on Pete."
I don't even complain anymore about dogs,
just let them hop on in.
He tells me where to go,
says he's lucky to remember where he lives
after the doctors cut the top of his head off
and took out the plum-
sized tumor,
then put it back on
like the lid of a pumpkin.

"It didn't grow back right, and so now
there's this place where it's just skin
over my brain, you can feel it
but you wouldn't want to.
I was in the hospital for a year and a half, lost
everything, my house, my job, even
my wife, she took all my money, but we're
still friends, I don't
blame her. Large chunks
of my memory are gone and she deserves
better.
Of course I can't drive now, I'd probably
kill somebody,
and I don't want to do that.
There are seizures, too,
and all kinds of shit
and now the doctors tell me they've got to
go back in again.
I can't ask the taxpayers to pay anymore

for me, it's not their fault,
it's no one's fault, sometimes there's
no one to blame."

We pull up to a vacant lot
carpeted with dead grass and broken glass
in the desert sun.
He tells me he lives in the corrugated
tin shed back there in the corner.
"It'll be ok until whoever owns the place
finds out," he says. "Don't get sick
brother, whatever you do."

He doesn't want to get out
of the air conditioned cab, so I don't
say anything.

"Look at this dog," he says scratching
its ears. "He's
so quiet you probably forgot he was here
didn't you? He's a good boy. I found him
when he was a pup, he just
showed up one day, poor little
fella."

In fact I did forget the dog was there. I've
never seen a dog so quiet.
I raise my head to the rearview mirror
and the dog seizes me
with his brown moon eyes
sitting on the seat like a child
who has matured beyond his years,
so well-behaved and tranquil
you think he must have come
from another world altogether,
tilting the gift of his head
into the man's fingers.

SYRUP

She's half Yaqui
half Huichol

reaching up
in a white summer dress

to pick mesquite pods from the tree
to boil for syrup

and my loins
lean
into the onion morning.

Later she undresses
and feigns bashfulness

showing me
her perfect brown ass

the syrup on the stove
bubbling
like a hundred forgotten
Mexican gods
hiccupping below the surface

and I realize
right at this moment
what is happening

really
is
happening.

BROKEN WINDOW GLASS ON THE PAVEMENT

diamonds
the car thieves
left behind.

MISTER BUBBLES

Each afternoon at the end
of my shift driving the taxi
I get the vehicle washed.

I go to the drive-thru car wash
where taxis get a
discount:
3 bucks.

I give the front-guy 3 bucks and drive
around back
and the Mexican guy waves me
closer
making sure I get my wheels in
place
always waving impatiently
COME ON, COME ON, LITTLE MORE, MORE, MORE, then he
puts his hand violently in the air
for me to STOP, NOT AN INCH
FURTHER, as if I have narrowly
avoided disaster.

Then he points to the sign which I know
by heart:

WINDOWS UP
CAR IN NEUTRAL
HANDS OFF THE WHEEL
FEET OFF THE BRAKES
WINDSHIELD WIPERS OFF.

And they have the instructions in Spanish
too.

Then the tracks grab my wheels and start
moving me into

the dark tunnel
with the yellow sudsy soap spraying all around
and the big loud brushes crashing against the sides
and the big heavy cloth flaps slapping down from above
the cacophony in which I somehow relax
and feel at peace
usually for the first time all
day.

Sometimes I do a bit of paperwork
under the dome light
adding up my numbers for the day
during those 3 or 4 minutes I am
in there
but often I just lean back and close my eyes
during that slow 50 meters where I am carried
and have no control or responsibility
and as the car is cleaned
it is like I am cleaned, too.

And soon I can see the light
at the end of the tunnel
as the clear water rains down
rinses off the grime
and the roaring blowers blow me dry
like jet engines
and then it all goes quiet
and I can see the Mexican kid standing there
at the finish
he rubs me down with his rag
like a boxer
his hands are fast and kind
and he gets my rearview mirrors
and some hard-to-reach places.

And when I'm finally birthed out

onto the pavement again
into the afternoon sun
he gives me a pat
looks at me and gives me the thumbs-up
which means I am free of the grip
of the machine
and I can get going

into the honking stinking mess
of the city streets
where the dust will settle
over everything

but where for a few
short miles
I shine.

FOR YOUR TROUBLE

The experience of taking a cab can vary greatly.
It can vacillate from an absolute nightmare
to a most pleasant and
even beautiful
experience.

Some cab drivers will make you feel
warm and cozy
like you're something special
and their cab will smell like
Bath & Body Works
and they will teach you about the history
of the city
and the geographic surroundings
and the culture
and they'll listen to your stories and
laugh at your
jokes
to the point where sometimes the cab ride
is the best memory you have
of visiting a foreign
city.

Other times, however, you'll get a driver
who's mama never taught him how
to clean his ass

who tailgates, who answers each question
you might have with
"Dunno"
who has road rage
who takes you the long way to
rip you off.

I've heard of cab drivers who carry
their pet snakes with them

or stop by their girlfriend's house to
"grab something real quick."

Or you'll get a driver who wants to ask you
uncomfortable questions
about your religion or politics
and wants to argue
or "debate"
or the driver who is barefoot
or who literally lives in his cab
you can see his dirty shorts on the floorboard
the seat sticky from his
wet dreams.

Or you might get the kind of cab driver
who likes to FIXATE on you
in the rear-view mirror
instead of watching the road
and you can see his beady little eyes
as if he remembers you from somewhere
and doesn't like you
as if he wants to take a hard right
and leave you
out in the desert.

Or you might get the kind
who complains the whole way
of his lot in life
the fact that nobody tips
and all his bills
and 9 kids
and the bad deal existence has
thrown at him.

Or, ladies, you might get the kind of driver
who suggests you could pay him

with something besides
money.

The sad thing is
a bad cab driver might once have been
a good one
and a good one might
snap any day now

so tip the good ones well
and the bad ones less
but if you don't tip
at all
you are flirting
with darkness.

LACK OF IMAGINATION

Whenever I think
my life is not up
to snuff

I try to imagine
who I would want
to trade places with

and I can never think of anyone.

WHICH WAY IS UP?

His name is Andrew Nueheisel
and he climbs into my cab
at La Paloma
the fanciest resort in town, he's maybe
45 years old.

HOW'S IT GOING? he asks, in a voice
that shakes the cab.

Oh, not too…I try to answer.

HAVIN' A GOOD DAY?

It's been…

HOW LONG YOU BEEN IN TUCSON? YOU FROM AROUND
HERE?

I moved here about…

WHAT ARE THOSE MOUNTAINS OVER THERE?

Those are the…

DO YOU LIKE LIVING HERE? IS IT HOT HERE
IN THE SUMMER? I'LL BET IT'S
HOT HERE IN THE SUMMER. I DON'T
THINK I COULD TAKE IT.

Yes, it's…

WHAT DRIVES THE ECONOMY HERE? WHY DO PEOPLE
LIVE HERE? WHERE'S
MY PHONE?

Well we have the university…I think you had it
when you got in…

OH HERE IT IS. I THOUGHT I LEFT IT
AT THE HOTEL. THAT WOULD HAVE BEEN TERRIBLE.

Good thing…

YOU HAVE A LOT OF MOUNTAINS HERE. DO YOU LIKE
MOUNTAINS?

Sure.

WHAT DO YOU LIKE ABOUT THE MOUNTAINS?

I like that they're mountains?

I SEE A LOT OF BICYCLISTS AROUND HERE. ARE
THERE A LOT OF PEOPLE WHO LIKE TO RIDE
BICYCLES AROUND HERE?

Guess so.

HOW COME I WONDER?

Good weather, I guess.

WHAT'S THAT BUILDING THERE? DARN, WHERE'S
MY PHONE? DID I
FORGET MY PHONE? OH HERE IT IS. WHEW!

That's the old mission church, if you're
interested…

WHAT'S "TUCSON" MEAN? HOW FAR AWAY IS
MEXICO? WHAT ARE THOSE MOUNTAINS THERE? WHICH WAY
IS NORTH? IS MEXICO OVER THERE BY THOSE
MOUNTAINS?

So, I said, what do you do?

I'M A PSYCHIATRIST. THERE WAS A CONVENTION
THIS WEEKEND. I LED A MEDITATION EACH MORNING
AT LA PALOMA. IT'S GOOD
TO FOCUS. WHAT'S "LA
PALOMA" MEAN?

It means, "The dove."

DARN, WHERE'S MY PHONE?
ARE WE THERE YET?

I want to reach behind me and smack him
but instead just look out
at the mountains

and blur my eyes.

OUR MORNING TRAIN

My wife and I get up at 3 o'clock in the morning
and get ready for work,
drive in together.
She drops me off at the taxi yard
and then she goes to work at
McDonald's.

It is dark in the morning and the streets
are mostly empty
and we are both tired
and feeling put-upon by
life, sipping our
coffee.

Along Aviation Highway
there are the train tracks
and each morning we look for the light
of the single eye of a train
coming through.
When we see a train we are both
happier somehow.

"There's the train," my wife says,
"Your favorite, now you won't
be sad."

"MY favorite?" I say. "It's YOUR
favorite, you just don't want to
admit it, the train makes you
all warm inside."

"No," she says, "not me, I am just happy
for you because I can see the light
in your eyes when you see
the train."

"Oh, no," I say. "You love that train,
Que nina!"

"Mira," she says, "There's the trenecito! Aren't you
glad?"

The "little train" she calls it
though it's not little at all, it's huge,
bigger than life, deadly,
going somewhere.

"There's your trenecito!" she says. "Aren't you
glad?"

And we go on and on and it is
funny
kidding each other, but the truth is we both feel better
when we see that train.

Maybe that train is destined for some
beach somewhere
in Mazatlan or
Kino Bay or San Carlos so far away
from this American drudgery, this train that goes
through our hearts
always heading in the opposite direction
and with such surety to its movement
and pride in its horn.

Maybe it just helps to see a bit of life
moving at this ungodly hour
besides us
knowing that there are other shmucks
awake and working
when the normal human being
wants to be asleep.

I don't know, but each morning
we look for the train

and when it does not come
we are both a little quieter

before that big
empty space.

WINE, POZOLE AND CLEAN AIR

I have wine, pozole and clean air.

I have a beautiful woman with eyes as bright
as a toucan's laugh.

I have 9,000 personalities
and the hundreds of eggs they lay every day.

I have truth like the thumb
of all things.

I have half
of two bodies
on a hot mattress
with crisp blue sheets.

I have siesta dreams
that make me sad
the afternoon can't last forever.

I have ancient blood around me
that shines like new.

I have this long hot desert
the cactus that rise so slowly
like they couldn't care less about love
or like.

I have my lies
that mesmerize me in my weakness
and my efforts that thicken
my watery soul.

I have moments of strength that come upon me
like a sudden storm
I have people that care

even if their care doesn't understand
I have people that will walk through fire for me.

I have so much that if I give it away
it becomes more
and if I hoard it
I become a hollow place
without even an echo.

FROM THE DIRT

Gave the maters a drink
the morning clear and hot and silent

and I keep turning my head
to see if someone notices me

even though I'm alone.
It's curious my self-sick desire

to be known
to be hauled on shoulders or pulled by burros

up mountains
fanning myself with feathers

and popping the eyeballs of dead men, of better men
into my mouth like fritters.

I cut my toenails and liken the discards
to crescent moons

admire my own feet and wiggle my toes
thinking myself sexy.

Mulched the peppers yup
god how slow they grow

but I will munch their juicy pulp
in sultry August

my teeth green
on a side-tracked road

to no kingdom
my toothpick compass failing me.

I smile at the sun
say Hola, Senor, que tal?

Shoveled the manure
into the sand

worked the peat into the clay
smoking a cigarette I rolled

massaging my sore neck.
So fast the sweet day closes.

My lizard tongue
snatches a bug from the air.

I swallow it
think love is like

a little man
on a little hill

singing a bolero
to a wild pig.

A POEM WRITTEN AFTER VIEWING SEVERAL YOUTUBE VIDEOS OF POETS READING THEIR PRECIOUS WORKS

You don't have to be old to dislike poets
or to want to send them to an island with starving crocodiles
where they can make all the YouTube videos they want
and tell us in their affected voices
about authenticity.

God
why did you give us
a pubescence
that lasts 300 years
why did you give us pencilly kids in dorm rooms
talking into me-phones?
Why did you give us boys who stroke their beards
like they've got pussies on their faces?
Why did you give us girls who say like
and look at us with eyes that don't think
but only want what they have not earned?
We are not offended, skinny pants
we are bored, we have seen you, like all men have seen
their pee-stained offspring preen and comb
like the painters of pre-Australia must have seen
like the petroglyph carvers of the Sonoran desert must have seen.

The artists seem to be nothing but pretention
and microphones.
They do nothing
to sharpen that cutting edge they love to speak of
in a world that worships brats
of all ages
in a world that worships mucousy hipsters
of all ages
in a world that worships anarchists of daddy's money
and the awe shucks lie of false humility.

Listen to them read their crap, heckle their faces off
tie them up like virgins for the slaughter

like the perfect offering to an Aztec god
praise them and praise them while slitting their throats
and hope their blood comes out red not snot-green
like a pheromone warning trail from the ant
who never comes home

before they become

grant recipients and tenure track faculty
teaching and preaching
giving workshops about the importance of character
against a sunset backdrop in Kauai

before they become

wine-sippers and pinky-typers
writing 2 hours each morning before yoga
zen practitioners
peddling their bikes to the coffee shop

before they become

editors of 7 different online
zines simultaneously

before they become

resident poets
sitting in chairs in perfectly ordered rooms
writing poems about Geronimo
or talking about Buddhism with great chasmic

pauses between lines

please   .

just end it now
I'm begging you.

DAY OFF FROM WORK

You don't put
deodorant on
and by the afternoon you realize
just how
much you
stink.

CARTAS DE AMOR

The other day I imagined Araceli died
and left me alone in this house
and I thought, that would be the end of me.
I had no idea how I would go on.
I thought about sitting alone here
writing letters to her ghost
a whole book of letters
in her Spanish language
even though I don't know it very well.
I figured she would understand me
even from the grave
like when we first met how we communicated nobody knows
not even us.

I made some notes about what I imagined
left the paper my desk
and when Ara came home from work she found it.

I came into the room and she was crying.
She thought I was writing a goodbye letter to her
thought I was leaving her
thought I was going to sell the house and go away.
It took me 30 minutes to convince her otherwise
and when she finally believed me
understood that I was thinking of writing an imaginary
book of letters to her after her imaginary death
well that didn't sit too well either
and though the tears stopped
she looked at me like she didn't know who I was

and was distant later in bed.

Best not to imagine your love dead
or to put literature ahead of life.
Best not to write certain things down

or if you do
burn them
or hide them
for some cold dark day.

THE PANIC BUTTON

On the left side of this taxi's dashboard
just below the steering wheel
is a little red button
called
the panic button.

You're supposed to push it
if you're in trouble
but don't push it unless it's
serious.
This button is only when you feel your life
is threatened.
Of course, it's hard to know these things
until it's too late
so really the little red button
is pretty much worthless
and just for show, something
to make you feel better.

Many cab drivers have been robbed or injured
or killed
and somehow the little red button
never played its part.

Sometimes when I am in my cab
alone
in a traffic jam somewhere
I feel a panic
rising in me
like an anxiety attack
and I feel my hand reaching toward
that little red button.
I want to scream out:
Help me, somebody, Jesus God! This is
all such nonsense. My life is being
bled from me and I am letting

it happen.
I have no idea what to do
how to fix it
how to feel whole, how to feel
meaningful, why is everything so
fucking dark and scary and
pointless?

But, I never
do it.

Instead I put my hand on
the steering wheel
and keep moving forward
to wherever the hell it is I am
going.

A FAVOR FOR THE STATE

I C-book a call on the cab's computer screen
and it's a medical voucher, shit-pay,
a favor for the state.

I call up the number and a guy answers
screaming into the phone:

"YEAH!"

"Yeah, I'm your cab driver, you still need a
ride?"

"WELL NO SHIT DUDE!"

"All right, I'm on my way."

"So, what's that mean? You gonna be here
in five minutes? An hour?"

"Your pickup is scheduled for
10:30, so it should be around then."

"ALL RIGHT!"

I get to the apartment building
and this BIG black guy is standing in the middle
of the parking lot, waving at me.

"WHAT'S UP DUDE!" he screams
as he climbs in the back.
He's a monster, muscular
and mean-looking.

"Not a whole bunch," I say.

"Shit it is HOT here! What the fuck you guys
do around here in AREEZONA for fun!"

81

"I like to ride my bike."

"What kind of bike you got, DUDE?"

"Fuji."

"A WHAT?"

"Bicycle."

"OH YEAH, I CAN DIG IT. I HAD ONE OF THOSE TOO
MAN, THAT THING JUST FUCKING FLEWWWW! Somebody fucking
ripped it off at the church I was going to though so now
I ain't got no wheels."

"Where you from?"

"Chicago."

"You like it here?"

"You got too many fucking PEEPING TOMS
dude! We ain't got no FUCKING PEEPING TOMS
in Chicago. Shit man I saw this little fucker
the other day trying to look into my
fucking window! When I catch him I'm gonna
break his fucking TEETH!
I MEAN I'M GONNA BREAK
EVERY DAMN ONE OF HIS TEETH!"

To emphasize this he hits his right
palm with his left fist about an inch behind my
head, SMACK!
I jump like a mule at a whip.

"I mean this fucking town is JUST FULL
OF PEEPING TOMS, I DON'T KNOW HOW YOU

STAND IT!"

I start to chuckle
and he goes off:

"I ain't a fan of PEEPING TOMS and I don't
appreciate you laughing about it, you're probably
A PEEPING TOM YOURSELF."

"Sorry, man, no, I'm not a peeping Tom."

"You ever want to deal with me you better just
deal with me to MY FACE. If I ever catch you
sneaking around my window man I'll fucking
KILL YOU."

My finger inches
toward the red panic button
on the lower left side of the dash near my knee, the button
that will send the police to my location
if I think I need it. I don't press it, though,
I just shut up, and so does
he.

When I get to the address
it's a doctor's office. I park and
he just sits in back steaming.

"GOD DAMMIT I HATE ALL YOU MOTHER FUCKERS!"

He stares at my face in the rear view
like it's all my fault
and then gets out still cursing.

He walks to the door of the doctor's office,
cups his hands around his eyes,
leans against the window
and looks in.

83

I TAUGHT MYSELF TO COOK

like any hungry boy
and I worked
like any fool.

I worked at a fish processing plant
in Bellingham, Washington
unloaded pollock and halibut from trucks
until my hands were swollen as a diabetic's.
I sliced heads off salmon
scored crab legs for governor's balls
and other slimy gruesome stuff
thigh-high rubber boots
rubber coat
rubber gloves rubber hat
one among hundreds of rubber covered workers
an army of walking condoms
ankle deep in fish guts and roe.
I came home smelling so rank my room-mates made me take off
my clothes outside
and hang them in the shed
enter the apartment in my underwear and go
straight to the shower.
Eventually I had to throw the clothes out.
One old fisherman asked me
why I wasn't in college instead of that stink-hole but
I had no answer for him.

I worked at a lumber mill after that
saw-lined conveyor belt what a dumb drone what a din
earplugs popping out of ears
like Frankenstein's neck bolts
foothills of scrap wood and sore forearms
sawdust up to your shins
trudging through it like yellow snow
couldn't smoke a cigarette anywhere near the place
college on the hill on the other side of town

all the graduates of back then
you can find now
saving the world on the Internet.

The only "net" I had back then was the one on my head
working in the kitchen at Chester's Fish and Chips
not moving up in the world
just kind of crab-stepping sideways and zig-zagging
along a rocky beach
where the water was too cold to swim
and reading Henry Miller in the college library.

I'd skip stones in Bellingham Bay
watch the phosphorous dance and play
the otters stick their heads out
the clams squirt their piss from the sand
like the automatic watering system at the golf course
where I worked next
mowing grass the second the dew dried
taming nature for knee-socked golfers.

The collection agencies and janitor agencies,
the gas stations,
drycleaners and day labor shacks,
bars and bookstores,
carwashes and phone sales,
jobs painting houses
jobs painting boats
jobs painting fences and curbs
I even had one job watching cement dry
at night

and on and on
more jobs than I had years on the planet
and every job I ever had
gave me at least one good thing
to take with me

until I found myself
age 43
sitting behind the wheel of a cab
like a little throne

riding my stubborn kingdom around
a strange desert
where I met a woman
like no other
and I put my head in her lap
and slept.

Worry worry
let me be
I'm going to make her
fish soup tonight
using a secret I learned along the way.

FIFTEEN MINUTES AND THE WORLD'S GONNA END

Matilde is a Yaqui Indian who I take to the grocery store
in my cab
hook nose dark skin small black eyes
maybe 60 years old.

Her grown son scowls at me from the doorway
of the huge posh house off
18th Street.

It's a free ride from the state voucher system for the poor.

On the trip we have a pleasant conversation.

Lived here all your life? I say.

Yes, she says, I've never been out of Arizona.

I tell her I went to Mexico once
on my last vacation 10 years ago
I went scuba diving there.

What did you see on the bottom of the ocean? she says.

I say,
Just a bunch of rocks and stuff.

She says, You didn't see any men
with tails like fish?

I say, no, ma'am, I did not.

Hmmm, she says.

When I drop her off at Albertson's
she tells me she will be ready to go home at 2.

Ok, I say.

I get back there for her at 2:15
she's livid
purple and puffing with rage
white man screwing her over again!
She gives me the business all the way home.
It's not right to make her wait!
Can't I tell time?
She's just as important as anyone else!
I drive and stare into the bright sunshine
and hope I'll just go blind and deaf one day.

I thought Indians were supposed to be patient.
I once read where the Papago Indians didn't measure time
couldn't conceive of measuring it.
To them a few weeks was the same as eternity.
Maybe that explains it.

Fifteen minutes and the world's gonna end.
Fifteen minutes and she's on martyr's rotisserie.
Fifteen minutes and now she's gonna miss her television program.
Fifteen minutes and her fat-ass scowling son's gonna beat me up
if I disrespect his momma again.

The thing about it is
I raced across town to get there for her
running yellows breaking speed limits risking my life
and livelihood
was damned pleased to arrive only fifteen minutes late
because my previous passenger wasn't ready
when he said she would be.
The address was wrong from dispatch
either from their incompetence or because the idiot
didn't even know his own address
and I got held up by a funeral procession
some dickhead had the gall to die
probably a white guy.

I keep quiet under Matilde's tongue-lashing
think about that brand new truck
I saw sitting in her driveway
like some shining mythical creature I've heard tales of
and how people
turn
and are not what they appear to be.

STUMBLING THROUGH THE DESERT LIKE A DRUNKEN JAVELINA

Messed up in the ho-hum a.m.
horns from a Mexican band whoring
for Tecate cans and the scaly wings
of Quetzalcoatl
but it's not as real
as my feet sweating in the ants.
You can rethink yourself all you want
but people can still tell when you've had plastic surgery
or are separated from your original god.

Time doesn't bat an eye
at the slick-faced youth
shiny as pennies in a baby's mouth.

How many pennies fill up
an old man's colon?
How many nickels clack
like rain on Tucson's Main Street?
How many dollars are folded
into crow's nests
or stuck like butterflies
on cactus needles?

Don't we all want a human being
to speak to us through the kaleidoscope
and take our hand?
Don't we all want a lover
to scratch our backs?
Don't we all want praise?
Don't we all want a straight stream
in the morning
not too yellow?

I swore to my wife
I'd leave it alone
but it won't leave me alone

thirsty and my ankles purple
as sliced tuna

the nearest fountain
moving farther away
a sorrowful hero
water squirting from his stone face
that keeps chipping off in bits and pieces.

ONE MORNING IT WILL RAIN GOLD

My face twitches
like the soul trying to jump
over itself.

One more morning and I'll have it
I'll be there
one morning it will rain gold
the world will know me
admire me
it will all seem worth it
I will sail into the future like a Viking ship
people will know my power my wisdom my great mind my
splendorous being

my tragedies sad and swollen
my desires sanctified.

I will wring blood
from intellectual turnips
buttress myself with moral squabbles
cleverness and lazy living
abstract my weakness into balloon animals
rub them on my hair
stick them to the walls.

I will amuse my bored peers and they will be plentiful
and even when death comes
a tip-toein'
it will be numbed to dreamland.

Look Mommy
I got me a A
I smart
I gonna be a artist
that's what smart people do
gonna read books and more books
gonna change the world
Mommy
you watch me.

HAPPY SMILING PEOPLE

The salamander the size of Godzilla
on the billboard at Alvernon and 22nd
tells me Geico's hiring
while I drive to Trader Joe's for wine
$39.26 a case.
You got to put up
with the chatty geek-mafia of employees
the pluckiest hippiest wage-slaves in Sproutstown
they're so freaking happy you'd think they were filming
Hee Haw
but it's worth it.

I get back in my car
9 a.m.
I catch a buzz for a few hours
then go pick up Araceli
at McDonald's.

She emerges crabby as an underpaid baby sitter
from the Ronny World bullshit
tosses a cold Big Mac at me
loosens her blue tie.

Thank God it's Friday, she says.

It's Thursday, I say.

Chingado, she says.

When you gonna find a job? she says.

Trader Joe's is hiring, I say, they need
some "Happy, smiling people."

She snorts
grabs my Big Mac and throws it out the window.

Did you get wine? she says.

Si, Bonita, I say.

You look sexy in your uniform, I say.

Ja! she says

but she's smiling now.

She IS sexy in that uniform
which she tears off at home
before she even reaches the bathroom
tells me to get her a glass of wine
jumps in the shower.

3 minutes later she's singing along
to the Mexican song on the radio
washing French fry crap
out of her long Mexican hair.

The afternoon is young.
A gecko slithers across the windowsill
and disappears
like a subtitle in a movie

gone too fast to read.

FACEBOOK CONVERSATION WITH A SMALL PRESS EDITOR AFTER 22 AND A HALF CANS OF BEER

Hello Joe, Happy Birthday.

Hello Mather, how are you?

Oh, like you care, Joe.

What's that supposed to mean?

Well, you never say hi to me on Facebook.

Hey, I'm busy. I'm not always on Facebook. Lots of irons in the fire.

Your Facebook light is always green and that means you're there, right?

Well, kind of. I mean, I'm here but I'm not here. I go in and out.

I see. But I notice that you make comments on other peoples' threads.

That's when I'm not busy.

Right, right.

Well, nice talking to you.

Be honest, it wasn't that nice.

No, it wasn't.

You know, Joe, sometimes I get tired of waiting 6 or 8 months for your mail replies to my submissions. I know that sounds rude.

Well, Mather, me and my friend get together and read the submissions, it's fun for us. We get together at the bar every six months and read them. You know, for fun.

I'm glad it's fun for you, but it's no fun waiting. Waiting sucks.

You're so impatient.

I mean, you never know what will happen tomorrow, and it's nice to feel that someone appreciates you.

Sorry, but lately we've been busy with our chapbook contest.

Oh, your contest?

You know, it's how we pay the bills.

I'll bet it's fun, too.

It is, we have fun with it.

I don't have any bills myself, my life is all comped.

Well, nice talking to you, Mather, hope you take your meds.

Thanks, Joe, I appreciate it. Just one more thing.

Yes?

Take my submission and stick it up your ass.

Well, Mather, that's no way to talk to an editor.

I'm sick of it, Joe.

Have it your way, Mather, your loss.

Hey Joe, hey Joe.

Yeah?

Happy birthday.

It's not my birthday.

It's not?

No.

Shit, then who am I talking to?

I don't know, Mather, you're drunk.

Is that why my ears are ringing?

No idea, I'm not a doctor.

You're not much help to me, are you, Joe? If that's really your real name.

Afraid not. Anybody ever told you you were an asshole, Mather?

A few times.

Well, you should listen to them.

I should, I should. It's just this thing about people, Joe, I mean, they piss me off.

How so?

Well, you know, they are so quick to be offended, so full of themselves. They think they're great, but I don't see the greatness.

You mean, um, like yourself?

Nailed it, Joe.

You know, Mather, I was just flipping through your submission and these are pretty good.

Really?

Yeah, I'd like to take one of these, or should I just stick it up my ass?

Hey, well, you know, I was just kidding around.

Sure, Mather. Ok, we'll take "HONK IF YOU LOVE FREEDOM" for next issue.

You're all right, Joe.

Usually we get together and read the subs together, my other editor and I, but in this case I'm making an exception.

Sorry to take the fun out of it.

It's ok. Gotta go now, Mather.

Hey Joe, hey Joe.

Yeah?

Love you.

PINOT GRIGIO ON MY JEANS

I marinate in memories
sad arrogant fool
loopy and insecure
as a booby bird
rolling a smoke in the Cro-Magnon dawn.

Maybe I should have done heroin
when I had the chance
or gone to Michoacan and lived in a cave.

Someone throws a quote at a wall
about the necessity of solitude
for the development of the intellect

ha ha
ah gad
it gets a hundred likes.

I stir the shit
I stir the turds

standing in a puddle of goo
not looking too hot.

What good is an intellect if all you can do
is throw quotes?
What good is an intellect if you freak your soul
at the slightest dissent
and drag your trailer of credits around everywhere you go?

My skull hurts
but I resurfaced the countertop yesterday
there's stuff for burritos in the ice box
I'm not crying behind a steering wheel

and the birds should start singing
any day now.

SITTING ON THE EDGE OF THE BED LOOKING OUT THE WINDOW IN THE MIDDLE OF THE NIGHT

It seems everyone corrodes and twists themselves
into their own anchor

even the pirate swimming in gold
even the white whale
even the newborn gull
even the dog in the fountain
even the philosophy professor
with his pension that would make you shit a brick.

What are we supposed to do, work in the dark
like Orwell's miners
lost in the hull of time, chip away at it
and come home to canned oysters
thank God

and when Death sails up
and peers at us with the acid pupils
of his cannons?

Afterlife?

Ask the filthy fly
ask the lecturers of the million religions
ask the stowaways of the soul
ask the ghosts
of sausages
ask the pickled octopi.

Our hearts are clocks
ticking under water
the sound of the waves like giant shoe horns
a torrential repetition
of the existential shush
brushstrokes of paint on a pot of blood

and my love floats
as she sleeps, her breath

eases us across this sea
coated in entrails

her foot twitches
as if at the touch of something
below,

she sees our end
in her dream

but I can only wake her
if I see light.

EDUARDO'S TWO CENTS

Eduardo Castillo is 51 years old
already uses a walker
shuffles out of his little leaning
house
groans into my cab
and I get the slow boat going.

Como esta? I say.

Oh, bad, hombre, bad and getting worse.
They operated on my leg
and my eyes keep closing on their own.
I don't feel sleepy but I can't stop it.
I get dizzy and my eyelids get heavy
and I keep falling all the time.

As we pass by the South Lawn Cemetery
on the way to his doctor
he looks out the cab window
at the waves of green grass over the dead.
The gravestones are lined up straight
shaded by the tallest trees in the desert
like masts of ships swallowed
in the night.

You might as well
just leave me here, he says, if you want
my two cents
these fucking doctors ain't worth a shit, god
damned worthless pendejos!
All they're interested in is grabbing your money
before you croak!

I give a nervous chuckle
even though I know
it's not a joke

fight the current
of traffic

do not dare to turn
toward the two pennies
sinking into his face.

A POEM FOR THE LAST MATCH

I disturb the copper worms
beneath the buckled sidewalks, worry over lullabies,

look slant-wise
at ugly men with beautiful wives,

pick at the word opposite, wonder
how luck lives with itself, how to light the wick

of the soul, to art or to fart, swivel my head
at the ping-pong of politics, make

do with day-olds, laugh at my gory particulars
and worser parts,

stutter at butter talkers, how
they sound so smooth and knowing, even breaking

wind with a cocky zest, the bringers
of deep-fried zingers, the never-

flustered, the handlers of snot-slick
automobiles, man-tans and cigars, bright

mile-long smiles, the other
lives so I may see and know and smell

their cinnamon wisdom,
but also to bow in deference

to low pants, patchouli-pits, knuckle tattoos, dog-shit
waterfalls, trustafarian fanfare, prefabbed

improv, pecker-grabbers, prenatal scenesters, self-crowned
outlaws, sixth grade nicknames and fixy

bikes. Sometimes the truly dead appear
healthier than many walking the streets, healthier

than my face in the mirror. I want to

reflect the sun like a belt buckle
on a bronco buster

while admirers down cups
of soda pop and yellow beer,

I want to be loved
and envied and feared and so much more

like wanting forever, useless
to want, useless to not want, the end

will come and it will
be blank as a cashier's forehead, no matter

how the bum on the corner
dotes about god with his cardboard sign

or that he calls me a saint
for a buck.

BILLS IN THE PICNIC BASKET

I hop barefoot across the august coals of Tuesday afternoon
to get my mail at the communal mailboxes
a quarter mile away at this thousand-holed
birdhouse for people.

Nothing but bills.

I remember when I was a kid my mom would get the mail
there was always something magical about the mail
I would ask her
What did we get?
I imagined something wonderful would come one day
something that would change our lives
rip us out of our dull routine
make my mother smile
maybe money or a ticket to another world
or city
maybe something from Ed McMahan
or an invitation to *The Price is Right*
but my mother would always say the same thing:
"Just bills."
She'd throw them into a picnic basket by the table
and start boiling
the same old macaroni.

I always thought it was somehow my mother's fault
that all we got was bills
that she must be doing something wrong to be so unhappy
and when I was 18 years old I got the hell out of there

I ran like the wind

but I learned pretty quickly
that it wasn't my mother's fault at all
the world was a sick and stupid place that cost too much
and ate good people alive.

I walk back towards my apartment this Tuesday afternoon
35 years later

smell the fire of someone's barbecue
a little altar there in the middle of the grass
a rib-eye smolders
the tongs lay just so
a brown bottle of something with the cap off.
Where is the chef?
Maybe he went inside to take
a piss or get the salt shaker or maybe
the phone rang.

I clutch my stack of bills and want
to toss them into the barbecue coals
disrupt this peaceful little still-life
I put my bills close to the heat
smell the charred meat see the blood seeping out
god it would feel so nice to watch
this bullshit go up in flames
but what then
more would come
they'd shut off my utilities
it wouldn't solve anything.

Instead I put the bills in my pocket
think of the macaroni waiting for me

think of my mother
eating dirt

I grab that steak off the grill

hot
hot
hot

toss it back and forth in my bare hands

run like the wind.

LEAVING MY EX-LIFE

I'm happy tonight.
A tequila bottle bends
like a pencil shaking
in Mayahuel's fingers.

I suck the last lime
of Mazatlan

grimace

then roam to lay the ghost of me
through a sugarless chocolate breeze.

The stars have all lined up
like dominoes
made from the teeth of lost people
and fall flat to sleep
like the clicks of insects that suddenly go quiet
when I walk by.

Happy tonight
pressed into the present
all the words in the world slurred together
like the barking of coyotes at the door.
I open up to let them in—
they bound off like thick-hided fish
in fur jelly.

Happy tonight
set down by a river of gravel
which flows so lazy only the lizards can hear it
the wise old lizards eating ants
like lines of drop candy
on their way to Tumacacori
hill.

Happy tonight
this night of music
numbed by the million opinions floating like laughing gas
that disappears before it reaches my ears, my ears
pinned like two extinct moths to a porous tablet
and I'm freed by the knowledge of my 8-year-old self
twisting on a sheet of tin.

The water table sinks and the javelinas crush
their musk into the dry hillsides
this dead happy all-willing soul
where nothing is flat enough
to be true.

I write "HAPPY" into the sand like a blind man
one letter on top of the other
as a scorpion crawls into my ear
scratches an unknown name on my brain
one letter on top of the other.

My soul is dust and ash
the only thing left to burn are my teeth
but I have no match
my torch drowned in rapture.

There is a crinkling in my head
like a child opening up a piece of brittle
or beetles eating
each other
but there is no pain except the idea of pain
a hollow rock in the floodplain
that nothing comes out of when broken
and the air smells like creosote in lightning
a rain that evaporates before touching
my face.

They say the leaves of the creosote bush are medicine
but I am not sick

no I am not sick
I am happy
tonight.

I sit on the pebbles of a
smashed self

and I do not want
anything.

DRIVING MY WIFE TO MCDONALD'S TO WORK THE BREAKFAST SHIFT

3:45 A.M.

I pat down my graying Teutonic cowlick.
She combs her long black Mexican mane.

I yawn
which annoys her

and then she yawns a second later
which annoys ME.

I yawn a little bigger.
She yawns bigger still.

I yawn the Grand Canyon.
She yawns the Cañon del Cobre.

I yawn Conceptualism.
She yawns Realismo Visceral.

I yawn Chuck Wicks.
She yawns J Lo.

I yawn the balls of Morpheus.
She yawns Mictlancihuatl's wattle.

I yawn the Horse Whisperer.
She yawns 400 rabbits and the left-

handed hummingbird.

Finally we look at each other
and laugh.

She laughs a church
of chocolate bubbles.

I laugh quail flushed out of a
possum-bellied moon.

111

TOUGH SHIT

It's been tough around here lately.
We've been eating cactus from our yard.

It doesn't taste too bad
once you get the spines off and the baba slime out.

Eating cactus is supposed to slow your system down.
They say it's good for the sugar diabetes.
If I keep eating it everything will slow to a crawl.
I'll end up an old man
crouching in the dirt

unable to move
unable to wipe the baba from my chin.

I'll stick anybody who comes near me.
That will be my only joy.
I'll wrinkle and yellow in the sun
but I won't die.
I'll live for two hundred years.
Birds will make holes in me to have their families
and there won't be a damn thing I can do about it.

It's been tough around here lately

tough all over the world.

INTERVIEW WITH A POET

He begs his host and the audience
to be so gracious as to forgive him
because he's "rather hung-over"
from staying up all night reading Nietzsche
and drinking Maker's Mark
and hasn't had the fortune
of nipping off to the cappuccino stand yet.

Plus he's "positively exhausted"
from his two month reading tour
and needs to take a break
and let the
"well fill up."

A font of incomparable input
we sup it up like burros:
he tells us if you don't want to take the bus
on your reading tour
you can always take the train
or you could fly in an airplane
or drive in a car
and if you want to save money on food
it is best to eat in cheap restaurants
rather than expensive ones
(although occasionally it's nice to splurge).

He tells us the best way to get "free in your mind"
is to stop worrying about money
and it is assumed the subject of how his bills are paid
is either a matter of mystical serendipity
a rich woman
or a government check each month.

When he's not cutting poems
"to the bone"
he does fantasy football

supports angry females on social media
gives advice on the best headphones
alerts the populace to the presence
of Tom Waits and this strange new music
called the blues
acts as curator of newsboy caps
and guidance counselor
for hipsters.

He tells us his "ironclad character"
was "arduously attained"
and it took him "years of suffering"
to find his "voice"
which is odd because he's 26
and sounds like every
other stoner who ever rode a pony in the small press parade.

His fourth "full length" is coming out soon.
He has a "primary publisher" but he writes so "feverishly"
that he is obliged to occasionally "let"
other people publish his work.

He mentions 38 poets by name and then reiterates
how he detests name-dropping
and groups
MFA programs, too
well maybe not DETESTS because not ALL groups are bad
a poet needs to have a community
"generalizing is the protectorate of idiots"
and hate is simply not a word
in his vocabulary
suffice it to say he is on
the fence
when it comes to groups and MFA programs
while the evidence is still being tallied.

He reminds us that poetry
is something one must do in isolation
with a pen
or a typewriter
or a computer
or a magic marker
or a stick in the sand.
He himself has written poems in the margins
of sky-mall magazines
and on cocktail napkins
which proves a poet will write
because a poet must write,
period.

He advises youngsters to get back to nature
but not the roses and trees and deer and waterfalls
kind of nature
in other words, "write what you don't know"
except sometimes it is also good to
"write what you know."

His most recent book opens
with a Whitman quote
and if you don't know who Whitman is, well,
then you're still shitting yellow
in mama's wam-wam.

He tells us it is best to eventually get down
to prose writing
because the world just doesn't take poets seriously
due to the fact that civilization has been in decay
since the time of Bukowski
and perhaps even a bit before that.

He says he thinks it is important to
"keep literature dangerous"

and to illustrate this he explains that one of his chapbooks
is bound with birch bark
and stitched with tea-bag strings.

In closing
if you have even "the remotest interest in modern writing"
you will not miss his latest collection
though what it's called
I can't for the life of me
remember—

something with "blood" in it.

THE SWAN

Today while walking in the park
I see a swan in the bushes.

She's nesting
looking sad.

I say, "Hi mama, how's it going?"

She just looks at me.
She doesn't trust me
but I wouldn't hurt her
and I want her to know that.

I think about my wife
the child we almost had
and I want to bend down
and kiss this beautiful bird.

I take a step closer
and as I do she stands up
hisses at me like a snake.

What I see underneath her
in her nest
are 2 plastic water bottles
no eggs at all
just these 2 plastic water bottles

and then I jump back
as she charges—

white and furious
as the crest of a wave.

HULA HULA LOVE

Araceli thinks she's getting fat.
She puts her work pants on this morning
and the front button pops off
flings out and hits the wall.

She says she wants to start exercising
wants to buy a hula hoop.

I suggest walking or jogging or bicycling
or aerobics or swimming but all these
sound ridiculous to her.

So later she goes to the store to buy a hula hoop
but she's from Mexico and in Mexico they call them
hula hulas
so she's looking around the whole store for something called
a hula hula.
She asks some of the employees but nobody
knows what the hell she's talking about.
Finally she finds a stock boy who's from Michoacan
and he says, "Ah, si…"
and shows her where they are.

Holy shit she's sexy doing that thing in the living room
in nothing but her panties
and if you think you're getting older
try a hula hoop sometime.

I try it when she goes to the shower
place the ring around my waist and then try to swivel.
It just falls to my feet in
two seconds flat.
It's a hell of a lot harder
than making apple sopapillas.

I give up and hit the sofa.

I know my limits.
I may be old and fat but I've learned
some things:

wear stretch pants

you can't put socks on
a bobcat

and always
always always
tell your love
she's beautiful.

POSSIBILITIES BITTEN INTO THE SHOULDER OF 3 A.M.

Get born, seek mate, repo-dos, grill wings, melt in front
of miss universe

ball your socks, jack-off, don't weed whack
before 6, act zany

eat neat, look cool, suppose, hop hip
lope, oppose Hitler's roses, lean the way

the wind blows, support, feel sorry, fart
smartly, caramelize onions

choose paper, nix cook's special, send
kids loaded wishes, hate hate

talk right, break clean,
shame the wild, mount the tame

want nothing, have everything,
remember Rome, sift sand, sport baseball

caps, screw rice, buy American,
guffaw at sombreros, say it is

what it is, pinch lice, keep shrinks, plug in
water picks, scrub molars, know nice

smiles open doors
to Rorschach kill-floors, don't duck walk

heart the world, monitor moles
raise pinky, remember mother's

day, vomit quietly
omit pain, shun shit, shut tombs, pound chest

lock bike, don't call
collect, shoot straight, take in

a show, lick ice cream, tap glass once
sit in call-centers, taxi cabs, crap factories, white labs

fornicate for money, help people, pull strings
graph blackness, like Einstein's hair

jot numbers, make jokes, stare discretely, believe
tv, save, retire, wave spatula

get sauced, pretend to be
someone else, snicker, diddle, muddle, doodle

hold on to the holy trinity
of three friends, forget, go quietly

to bed, tread on he who tailspins, fuck
yourself, be forgotten, chew tripe

swallow down the right pipe
make pee pee, don't think

thinking makes death kinky.

BEAUTIFUL UP HERE

I pull up to Fry's in my cab
tired from the sensory-overload
of driving all day through this manic
and murderous maze of a city.
No cab driver likes grocery runs
because they are hardly ever going far.
People who take cabs to the grocery store
are almost always poor
and pissy because their ice cream
is melting.

I call the fare but he doesn't answer
and I get out and go grumbling
into Fry's.

I almost bump into this HUGE young guy
coming out
as I holler:

"TAXI FOR LARRY!"

And he says,

"That's me, I'm Larry."

He is at least 6 foot 8
400 pounds
could easily smash me
like a bug.
He's got a blind man's cane
and a little bag of groceries
and he's smiling.

"Oh," I say, "Pardon. Can I take
that sack?"

He gives it to me and I
walk him to the cab.

"Watch the curb there."

When he is in the cab he tells me where
he lives and it is a little farther
than the usual 5 dollar grocery
run.
It is a nice sunny day and he has
a blind man's kind but twisted
look on his round
pale face as he sits in the back.

"Nice day," I say.

"Yes."

He tells me the directions to his
house in a very precise manner
that I appreciate
because many people are vague in their
expression and directions
which make it easy to get lost
or take a stupid route.

We go up a hill into the desert
and the cactus are there and the ocotillo
with their little orange flowers
because it's rained recently.

"Damn," I say, "It sure is beautiful
up here."

I cringe after I say it
thinking it uncouth to say that to a blind man

who has never had the pleasure
of gazing at this desert loveliness
or the view of Tucson below
or the birds flying
in the morning.

But he doesn't take offense.
He just says,
"Yes, it sure is beautiful."

At his house he says,
"There's a palo verde tree there in front,
do you see it?"

"Yes."

"Park there."

He pays with a 20 dollar bill which he fishes
carefully out of his wallet
and which is folded in such a way
to let him know it's a 20
and I give him change
and he seems to trust me
not to rip him off
not to give him ones
instead of fives.

Then he gets out, thanks me, and feels
his way to his front door
with his cane and his little sack
and finds the doorway
which he barely fits through
and then shuts the door
behind him.

I close my eyes.
It is quiet sitting there in my cab
under the palo verde tree
on top of the hill.

Almost perfectly
quiet.

DON'T STOP

Not a straight line anywhere on her
she struts through the rectangular door
in white panties.

I stutter
like a man falling down a staircase
svelte brown body that would give
Picasso a stroke
black hair glistening mayhem
around her face.

I moan no
have mercy
I've still got scratches and bites all over my body
from yesterday.

I lift my hands from the typewriter
like it's a bank robbery.

Don't stop! she says.

I keep typing though the words shatter
like glass gloves.

She squeezes in under my desk like a cat trying to fit
into a shoebox
pulls my chair tight up under
the top of the world
undoes the fly of my shorts
takes out my cock and starts sucking.

I can't see but I can hear
the a cappella of a Sonoran mountain lion
bolting a jackrabbit in a grotto.
Her head bumps against the underside of the desk
like some kind of insane
spirit knocking to get out.

Don't stop typing! she says again.

The cadence of the keys mixes with the blood-pop
pull of the female carnivore.

I obey
fearing more the round-eyed bore
of those who would level existence
like a sand dune
who want to eradicate and condemn and ignore
a natural and intense polarity
people who write and write and write but never come
home:

I slide my chair back, yank her out of there
by her wrist
flatten her stomach onto the floor
climb on top of her, press my palms on her
rolling shoulder blades
lick her brown asshole like a sassafras-oiled
knot
and fuck her 15 feet across the cut pile carpet
to the wall.

And while she yowls and cries
and I yowl and cry

the teeth of the typewriter grin
in their skull.

AFTER TOO MANY BLOODY MARYS

The cut
on my dick
is in the shape
of a cross.

My wife
has devout
teeth

white
strong
clean

but not
without guilt.

THE SELF-CROWNED OUTLAW POETS

Keep poetry dangerous
says the poet with his middle finger
up in the camera
big bad beard
armband tattoo
MFA degree
and job as sensitivity trainer
at Geico.

Keep poetry dangerous
by starting Internet zines
and moderating out the negative comments
or by reviewing the work of your thousand friends
and calling everything
awesome and brilliant.

Keep poetry dangerous
by creating a cartoon character
pen-name
like Razor Sharps
or Vagabond Vicky.

Keep poetry dangerous
by jumping on every liberal
band wagon that stops at the co-op
by calling the cops on your neighbors
when they're arguing while you're trying to
pen your opus
by calling anyone who might disagree with you
a bully.

Keep poetry dangerous
by putting it on a T-shirt and selling it for 25 bucks
by putting it on a bumper sticker
by calling your typewriter a machine gun
by loading it

with crap
by screaming red-faced into the microphone every third
Wednesday at the Netherbrew.

Oh lordy, keep poetry dangerous
as kittens are dangerous
to balls of yarn
as Takeru Kobayashi is dangerous
to weenies.

The self-crowned outlaw poets
are only dangerous
to poetry
as they beat it like a piñata
and scramble for the dirty candy.

AND NOW THERE'S NO GOING BACK TO SLEEP

Araceli wakes me up at 4 a.m.
and kisses me goodbye
before she goes to work.

I sleep in on my day off.
It's raining in my dream
and a car alarm blares
and then at 6 o'clock my phone starts ringing
from the kitchen table.
Emergency, I think
get up
stumble around till I find it.
It's not a person calling, it's the ring of a reminder
that my wife has programmed into my phone
(I don't even know how to do that)
and there is a note on the screen:

REMINDER 5th ANNIVERSARY.

I look at the date on the bottom right hand corner:
July 30th.
Today, our fifth anniversary.
Shit, we'll have to go to dinner later.
I go back to bed.

10 minutes later I am dreaming of being
in some kind of race
where everyone knows the rules but me
when the phone starts ringing again.
I'm up and off to the kitchen again and it's the same
message:

REMINDER 5th ANNIVERSARY.

I mean, we're happy, aren't we?
We've got a good life.
She knows I love her.

I go back to bed
this time bringing the phone with me.
I am just into another dream where some strange voice
is about to tell me the meaning of life
when it starts ringing again:

REMINDER 5th ANNIVERSARY.

I can't figure out how to turn the phone off in my
half-awake state.
I press every button on it and finally
the screen goes black with an electronic "so-sorry"
wind-down sound that reminds me
of music they'd play on a game show
after I answer
the last big question wrong

and fail to win the shiny new car
for my hopeful wife

but instead must satisfy her
with a year's supply
of sunblock
and a gift certificate to Paco's Tacos.

GARY'S TREE

For years Gary parked his cab
in the shade of the tree in the corner of the parking lot
behind the Waffle House
on 22nd Street
when it got hot in the afternoon
and it was slow and he was tired
of driving.

Gary's 68
with a long white beard, one replaced
knee
and he walks with a cane, been
driving a cab for 36 years.
He can remember
when that tree behind the Waffle House
was small
and the Waffle House hadn't even been built yet.

Yesterday he told us other cab drivers

"Some fuckhead cut my tree down!
Now I got no place to go.
I'd like to take an axe
to that son of a bitch!"

And there are people who will say
Gary needs more courage
to live a fuller life
and there are people who will say
Gary needs to find another job
and anyway
it wasn't HIS tree,
it wasn't his PRIVATE PROPERTY,
he had no RIGHTS when it came to this
tree.

I guess that's true
but there aren't that many trees
around here,
it gets hot in the summer
under that sun
and Gary doesn't have much
to live for anymore.

And now he's talking
about killing someone
with an axe

and there isn't a cabby in the yard
who would stop him.

AFTER READING BRUCE EMBREE'S BOOK *ALL MINE*

5 a.m.

Today is the first day
after I quit my job.
I was worried a bit
about not being able to write.
All I've written about for 6 years
is my job.
I was worried I'd go crazy
with nothing to do
but a kind friend Rusty Barnes
sent me a book of poetry.

It was written by a guy who committed suicide
when he was about my age.
His work is beautiful and hilarious
simple and real and unpretentious
against all odds.

He wrote in a shack somewhere in Idaho
next to a wood burning stove.
He was hardly published at all in his life.
Hardly anybody knew him or his work
and still don't.

I was up half the night reading it.
I can't remember the last time that's happened.
I didn't have to get up this morning to work
but got up anyway.

This poet this man
who killed himself
in 1996
at the age of 47
has brought me to life again.

AVAILABLE

I quit my job cab-driving last week.
8 years driving the streets with that crooked outfit.
8 years in old number 85
ugly yellow beat-up auctioned-off
cop car
with the sputtering light on the top:

AVAILABLE.

She had pennies in the gas tank
black smoke when she started up
whining and groaning
up the sienna hills of Tucson.

It was my longest relationship
my twisted abusive love
ended with a drunken phone call
at 7 a.m
to an irate boss
with my slurred words:

"Don' care n'more!"

Now the sense of freedom
mixed with doom
checking the bank account
doing figures with a shaky hand
trying to relax
and understand things.

I go for a walk today
to lay the ghost and take the sun
and while I'm out I see old number 85 sitting at the Circle K
and stand across the street staring.

Shinier, sleeker
new tires
but it's her, no doubt about it.

A creep comes out the doors of the Circle K
opens a pack of smokes
climbs inside her
checks himself in rearview mirror
my mirror
backs out without looking
cuts somebody off pulling out
onto 22nd Street.

I watch her head west
no black smoke anymore
no hesitation
new tires.

Bye bye
old gal.

ON MY WAY TO THE UNENJOYMENT OFFICE

The stinking wet road that stretches
all the way to the unemployment line
starts right there at your feet. I stagger

through alleys of anger and stupidity
and everything I find I pick up
and stack on my back, thinking there will be
a use for it someday.

I simper before rippled reflections
in storefronts and across parking lots

wide as tundra. I stand heavy
and I listen
with my procedured-to-death eardrums
and smile
through my pride's gapped teeth.

My hollow cheeks don't know who they are anymore
and my eyebrows have given up
and if I was asked I could not reply to love

but I am not asked
the same way I do not ask
for anything more emotional
than a dollar or a cigarette
and even though I know such things
on being handed over can be
answers at times, I also know they are held out

far from the heart.

I am a beggar
at the bottom of a well.
People drop me coins, but I can see in their faces
they don't know
what to wish for.

138

KINO BAY OR BUST

You've got a Mexican beach on the brain
in your brother-in-law's house in Hermosillo
after the 5 hour drive from Tucson
trying to talk everybody into going to Kino Bay
only an hour and a half away

but Miriam doesn't want to go
Kareli doesn't want to go
nobody wants to go.

Well Colo wants to go and your wife wants to go.
Ok now Miriam wants to go just let her paint her nails first
and call her boyfriend.
Can you pick up Pablo?
Sure you can pick up Pablo.
And, pues, if Miriam's going then Kareli wants to go too
so you load up the minivan.

Now your wife's father comes over and he's 73 but he wants to go.
He hasn't been to the beach in 30 years
and finally you're off with a car full
in the hot bright sexy sun
no lane lines on the road
open-for-interpretation speed limits
Mexican music on the radio
dodging pot holes and listening to the wonderful chorro
of Spanish chatter.

Halfway there you've got to stop at a pueblo called
"The 12"
because everybody's thirsty.
Everyone gets out and you stand in the sun smoking while a
skin-and-bones drunken Indian with teeth like a shark
mumbles you out of 10 pesos
and when everybody gets back with their Gatorades
and lime-chile peanuts

the damn piece of crap car
won't start
just turns over and turns over
"prende, prende, prende!"
but no prende.
It's the battery!
It ain't the puto battery!
Shit and fuck and carajo and nos lleva la chingada!

You pop the hood and 3 Mexican guys come out of nowhere
dive in arguing and checking things.
The consensus is it's the fuel pump.
The fuel pump's gone fucked itself.
Pues what now it's Sunday no mechanic is open here.
Phone Ubaldo your brother-in-law
and Ubaldo calls Cacharpas the mechanic in the family.
Better to have a mechanic in the family than a lawyer, doctor or
liquor store owner
and they say they'll go get the part and come on out
from Hermosillo.

So you wait
the girls fanning themselves and texting on their phones
but not complaining.
This is just a normal thing in Mexico.
It's life what can you do
and you and the old man stand in the shade of the Oxxo market.
4 young Mexican kids have washed the car windows
with their little squirt bottles.
This dusty town of rocks and poverty.

A tiny Indian comes walking up barefoot through the shattered
glass
stands squinting at you with delirious drunken eyes
stands there and stands there
no physical threat only a spiritual intimidation.

You give him a dollar.
He never stops staring at you as he takes it
and you turn away
like from some boogie man in a dream.

There's a taco stand across the road with some plastic chairs.
You all trudge over
cars moving by honking like elephants in a war zone
cars so old you can't even identify them
cars made out of other cars
cars with no doors no hoods
cars with engines bared and hanging out like grotesque
mechanical tumors throbbing and dripping
in the heat waves
but somehow still running pistons still chopping
unlike yours sitting there gagging in the sun
like an idiotic gringo after a shot of bacanora.

The taco stand lady doesn't even want to stand up
but finally she does and dishes out a plate of the greasy
pork meat covered in flies
some corn tortillas
bottled orange sodas.
You ask her for forks and she just looks at you and walks away.
Scoop the meat up with your hands
choke down the tacos.
Everything smells like urine.

Another drunk lies on the sidewalk arms outstretched
more sun-burnt than Jesus ever was.
People step over him like a big banana peel.
A truck crashes into a utility pole 20 feet away
and you all jump and laugh and look at the smoke.
The drunks fall out of the truck cussing.
Your father-in-law says,
"This is a town without law."

And finally Ubaldo and Cacharpas the mechanic show up
with Cacharpas's wife and 2 kids
and a cooler in the trunk full of Tecate beer.
You all push the car over to a shady spot
on the edge of an open field
thinking, if that was only the sea, why can't that be the sea
and Cacharpas checks and shit god dammit
they've brought the wrong part

and they have to go BACK to Hermosillo again.
Another 2 hour wait
and you drink beers and play Frisbee with the kids.
You've brought the frisbee which they call
a "platillo volador"
another name for a UFO.
They have never even touched a Frisbee but catch
on quick after 2 hours
in the dirt and rocks and broken glass and dog shit
and you laugh
and your wife joins in, hell it's not too bad
kind of fun after all
and as you toss the beer cans on the ground
the Indian kids scurry over to pick them up for money

and finally our saviors get back with the new fuel pump
Ubaldo and Cacharpas still arguing
"I TOLD YOU TO BUY THE OTHER ONE!"
"CALLETE! FUCK YOU!"
and the god damned gas tank has to come off
full of gas of course like a drunk's bladder.

The sun is going down.
Ubaldo pulls his car up close and uses the headlights.
Nobody watches the sunset, all eyes trained on this mechanic
working his magic.
The gas tank comes down finally and he gets it out from underneath.

142

Shit, got to get that gas out of there, give me the hose!
Cacharpas sucks on the hose to get the gas flowing
into a bucket.
"You gonna kiss your wife now?" everybody laughs.
Shit look at this gringo gas! It's so clean
it looks like lemonade!
They put the gas into Ubaldo's car, he's almost empty.
"Now the radio's gonna play gringo music!"

Cacharpas slips in the new fuel pump
gets it on tight
bitches and moans and laughs as he gets the tank back on under
the car.
Where's the last screw?
You all stand around kicking the dirt looking for the lost screw.
Finally your wife finds it
and then Ubaldo gets in behind the wheel, crosses himself
and tries to start it:
"prende, prende, prende!"

and it starts!
Everyone cheers!
Cacharpas the hero!
A truck slows down as he passes you all
then backs up and slams into another truck parked on the street.
"Need any help?"
Naw, it's ok, gracias!
He takes off again
not worrying about the truck he just crashed into.

You pay Cacharpas with pesos your wife has earned
from selling make-up and old furniture
buy some more beer and some more gas and think,
Damn, time for bed
but hell no Ubaldo makes a U-ee
heads for Kino Bay and you follow along

letting the tide take you.
There's no use arguing or worrying
eyes bleary in the oncoming headlights

and in another 45 minutes you roll into Kino Bay
quiet and dark
and the seafood restaurant where you wanted to eat crab tostadas
is closed
so the women buy stuff at the only place in town still open
and make bologna sandwiches
and crackers with cream cheese
which they simply call "Philadelphia"

and you all walk down to the cool sandy beach
white caps glowing in the dark
blood-curdling blackness where the sea meets the night
and what lurks out there
and the sound of it and the smell of it and the stars

and the kids jump in the water like goofy mer-brats
and you drink a few more beers
and get your feet wet
and kiss your wife
and think about sleeping right there
how nice that would be
and you just know you're gonna be sore tomorrow
from frisbee of all things.

You're getting old.
It's sad and kind of funny
and your father-in-law says
"Kino Bay has changed since 30 years ago"
and you pat him on the shoulder

and throw the frisbee to the arms waving
in the sea.

THE THUNDER

I want to put those cab-driving days behind me
but I can still hear the thunder
of the cab rolling
over railroad tracks...

I still think the most comfortable place to read
is in the seat of a parked cab
with my foot out the window.

I left part of myself at every stop I ever made
and I took a part of every fare
into me

but it was mostly boring
even the whores were snobs
the drug addicts so nervous and worried
and dumb.

I hated the drunks most
college drunks or old stinky drunks
drunks that pissed on the seat or threw up
or drunks who thought they were funny

and then there were the sick people god
the sickies the poor sickies
amazing the shitty luck some people have it's sad
but you get tired of being sad
you get tired of feeling sorry
sometimes you just want the sick and damaged people
to go away and die alone
like cats under rocks in the desert
yes you get cruel and it's nothing to be proud of
just self-preservation
I understand the jaded faces of emergency room nurses
the cool distance of doctors
the whining masses will claw at you
until you're sick too.

I got out of it
am I intact I don't know I don't think so
I know I'm haunted by ghouls
of lost barrios
pothole souls
pothead grins vacant with stories that trail
off into glossy-eyed dead-ends
no outlets
wrong turns a way of life
and one-ways
trips with no returns
no blow jobs for fares
no hot blonds looking to love me
life is not a movie.

Most of the time when you're driving a cab
or doing any other kind of job
you're just thinking
"Where will this end?
Where will it stop?"

One time I did see a girl walking down the street
in broad daylight
with no shirt, tiny shorts, barefoot, svelte as a fawn
she was smiling
at Dodge and Flower
young and beautiful
but she didn't need a ride
not even for free
she knew where she was going
I imagined it was someplace glorious

and I watched her walk
for a few moments

and I can still hear the thunder...

THE FIREFLIES OF IOWA

My mother has fixed
her house up the way she always
wanted it, took her
25 years, as long
as I've been away.
Wood floors,
furniture that still smells new,
kitchen appliances show-room shiny,
fussily decorated bedrooms
nobody sleeps in, clocks around
every corner
ticking in unison, every hair-raising minutia
sewn up
down to the special-order sheaths over the
tissue boxes.

My wife Ara and I sit on my mother's back porch with her
in the Midwest evening
the sky purple as a pickled beet
and I wonder aloud
where all the fireflies are.
When I was a kid there were thousands of fireflies
on summer nights
and I wanted Ara to see them. She's from Sonora,
Mexico, where we live now
and she's never seen a firefly.
We sit on my mother's porch and watch for them
like some long awaited comet shower
and we tell stories
and remember.
We talk about the other houses we lived in
which somehow seem more real
and we talk about my father
and the insanity on the other side
of the family
2 cornfield-filled counties

south.

My mother doesn't know
what happened to all the fireflies, they just
don't come around anymore.

As kids we used to put them in bottles
or tie string to them,
smash them on rocks and paint with them,
rub them on our faces and hands,
sprint in the dark like giggling barefoot spooks.
There were so many of them flooding the sky
blocking out the stars, we figured
they'd always be there, like so many things we figured
wrong.

When mom and Ara go inside
I sit for a while
alone in the silence
and guess what,

a single firefly

zigzags through the dark back yard
blinking tiredly in the mulberries.

It may as well be
the last one in town,
the last one in the world, for all
the light it gives.

ACKNOWLEDGEMENTS

Rattle, Hanging Loose, Busted Dharma, Blue Hour, Nerve Cowboy, Boyslut, Samizdat, Slipstream, Poetry Quarterly, American Dissident, Full of Crow, Words Dance, Gutter Eloquence, Regime, Rusty Truck, Revolution John, Four Chambers, Chiron Review, My Favorite Bullet, Backlash, Frigg, Misfit, Horror Sleaze & Trash and *W.I.S.H.*

* 9 7 8 1 6 3 0 4 5 0 4 1 0 *